BRITAIN IN PICTURES
THE BRITISH PEOPLE IN PICTURES

BRITISH PORTS AND HARBOURS

GENERAL EDITOR

W. J. TURNER

*

The Editor is most grateful to all those who have
so kindly helped in the selection of illustrations,
especially to officials of the various public
Museums, Libraries and Galleries, and
to all others who have generously
allowed pictures and MSS.
to be reproduced.

BRITISH
PORTS AND HARBOURS

LEO WALMSLEY

WITH
8 PLATES IN COLOUR
AND
23 ILLUSTRATIONS IN
BLACK AND WHITE

WILLIAM COLLINS OF LONDON
MCMXLII

PRODUCED BY
ADPRINT LIMITED LONDON
*
PRINTED
IN GREAT BRITAIN

LIST OF ILLUSTRATIONS

PLATES IN COLOUR

BLACK AND WHITE ILLUSTRATIONS

BONZO'S HOUSE, FILEY
Water colour by Sir Muirhead Bone

M Y father, an artist, was born and bred in Liverpool, but when I
was very young he emigrated to a small fishing village on the
Yorkshire coast near to Whitby, where he thought he could
keep himself and his family by painting water-colour sketches of local
beauty spots and selling them to the summer visitors, and at the same time
continue his more serious work " in oils," which in time he enthusiastically
believed would bring him fame and fortune.

Dad had no hankerings for the city and the life he had left. If fame
and fortune were destined to elude him, the sea and cliffs and moors, the
unspoilt beaches, the quaint village streets, the fisherfolk themselves and
their lovely cobles were for him an inexhaustible inspiration and delight.
Mother, too, if she found the domestic arrangements of a damp and
dilapidated fisherman's cottage rather trying at times was a true country
lover, and only on very rare occasions expressed a longing for what she
called " the rush and flow of souls." But both of them often talked about
Liverpool. I would listen with great interest and a great envy to mother's
descriptions of its wide and busy streets with electric trams running along

7

them, of shops so vast that you could get lost going from one department
to another, of St. George's Hall, and the Walker Art Gallery and the
Museum and the Overhead Railway. More exciting still, and breeding
a wilder envy, were her descriptions of the Floating Landing Stage, the
ferry steamers passing to and from Birkenhead and New Brighton, the
big ships coming in and out, the Docks, miles of them, full of ships unloading merchandise from all over the world. One day, when Dad's ship
came in (I took this literally as a Spanish treasure galleon, but for Dad it
meant the acceptance of his first " oils " by the Royal Academy) we were
all going back to Liverpool for a holiday, and I would be able to see these
things for myself. Every night when I said my prayers I used to add a
special postscript imploring that Dad's ship would come in soon!

True that Whitby, where we would go for a day's outing whenever
mother could scrape up enough cash for the railway fare, was a fascinating
place. Once ranking sixth among the shipbuilding and shipowning
ports of Great Britain (when Newcastle was little more than a quiet market
town on a practically un-navigable river) Whitby had passed her industrial hey-day. Sail had long since given way to steam, wood to iron.
Her numerous yards, where some of the stoutest of England's fighting
and merchant ships were built, including the famous exploring brigs of
Cook and Scoresby, were closed or derelict. One of them, the Whitehall
had changed over to iron, and had actually built several small steamers.
But the yard was too remote from the furnaces and foundries of the Tees,
Wear, and Tyne to compete with the tremendous shipbuilding industry
that had arisen there, and I was too late to see the launch which was to
mark the final closing of Whitehall. Still, Whitby's wooden ships had
been built to last. While most of the local owners had put their money
into steam, irrespective of where their new ships were built, several held
out obstinately against the changed fashion. There was still a lucrative
coast trade in Newcastle coal, and as one of the old Whitby graving docks
remained open there was usually one or two of these old-timers in port.
I could have spent hours in this dock watching the sailors at work on their
ship, which would be high and dry, with its hull supported from the dock
wall with great wood beams. Some would be scraping her planks, others
caulking the seams with oakum and pitch that was melting in a cauldron,
filling the air with a lovely tarry smell. A brig like the *Enterprise* did not
look quite so good in dock as it did when it was afloat with all its sails
set ; yet you could get closer to it, and see every detail of the rigging.
As well as *real* ships there were plenty of fishing craft in Whitby ; cobles
and luggers and ketches ; and in summer the harbour would be crowded
with Scotch, and East Anglian, and Cornish herring boats, their brown
sails unfurled and hanging limp from their masts to dry, their nets draped
over the quay-side rails, their crews standing about the fish market,
speaking what was for the local fishermen, and for me, an almost foreign

A MAP SHOWING THE CHIEF PORTS, HARBOURS AND COALFIELDS OF GREAT BRITAIN
Drawn by F. Nichols

tongue. All these men wore differently patterned guernseys, according to the ports they hailed from. Some wore hard-felted sou'westers, others Tam-o'-Shanters, and brightly coloured scarves. And many of the older men had gold rings in their ears and long hair, so that to me they looked like pirates. Those trips to Whitby in which so many valuable minutes were wasted by mother in shops, were always too short and too far between, and they only served to make me yearn stronger for that long-promised visit to Liverpool.

It came at last, when I was ten years old, not because Dad's ship had come in, but because poor mother got scarlet fever, and I had to be packed out of the way. Fortunately she was not dangerously ill, or my excitement might have been mingled with more than a tinge of home-sickness and foreboding during the long train journey I made in the company of my Aunt Emmeline, who had come from Liverpool to fetch me. She was much older than mother, dressed in black with a very severe face, and she spent nearly all the time reading the Bible, or telling me to be a good boy, and she was not a bit interested in the things I saw through the carriage window, and although she had lived all her life in Liverpool she did not seem to know anything about the docks or ships.

I was to discover, although the full significance of it did not dawn on me until the next day, that she lived in West Derby, miles from the waterfront, in a gloomy house in every room of which were hung religious pictures or texts ; that both she and Uncle James (who was a sort of clergyman, only he did not wear a round collar) thought of nothing all day long but religion, and the converting of the black and yellow races to the Christian faith. It seemed that Uncle James had wanted to be a missionary, but that he had not been healthy enough to go abroad so he made up for this by preaching and writing. He read the Bible and prayed for more than half an hour before breakfast next morning ; he said the longest blessing I had ever heard at dinner time, although there was scarcely anything to eat, and no pudding at all ; in the afternoon I was taken to the Mission Hall (where he preached on Sunday) and although it was empty we all sat down on a hard wooden form while Uncle said another prayer, and when we got home Aunty took me into the garden, which had very high brick walls, and told me I could play, only I must be very quiet, as Uncle would be writing a sermon in his study. When, after a tea marked by still another blessing, I dared to suggest that I would like to go and have a look at the docks, both of them were horrified. Apart from the docks being dangerous, Uncle said, that part of Liverpool was not at all a nice place for a little boy to be taken to. The men who worked there and the sailors from the ships were a very rough lot. They used bad language, they drank and brawled. There was one street down there called Scotland Road where there was a public house at every corner. The whole place was a haunt of iniquity and sin.

SHIPPING ALONGSIDE THE WEST INDIA DOCKS, LONDON
Lithograph by W. Parrott, 1813-1869

No. He and Aunty would take me a nice walk to West Derby village, which was very pretty, and later on, if I was very good, he would read to me out of a missionary magazine, a story of how little boys and girls in an African village were being taught about the Word of God, and the True Light of Salvation.

Well, I had had enough of this sort of thing at Chapel and Sunday School at home, and I was not going to be done out of something I had been looking forward to for years. Next morning Aunty was going to take me out for another nice walk (while Uncle got on with his writing) and as soon as she went upstairs to dress, I crept quietly out of the street door and then bolted as fast as I could go down the road, at the end of which, I had observed on yesterday's walk, there were tram lines ; and the first tram I saw bore on it the exciting legend PIER HEAD !

Pier Head, the Floating Landing Stage, the Mersey itself, as thick with real ships as Whitby harbour would be with herring boats in the height of the fishing season ! Even the ferry boats were exciting enough, but there were steamers six times as big as any I had seen before, passing so close I could hear the sailors on them shouting ; and most exciting sight of all, although she was anchored closer to the Birkenhead shore, was a monstrous ship with a black hull and white superstructure and four red funnels. I knew from a picture book I had at home that she was the *Mauretania*, the largest and fastest steamer in the whole world.

I was destined to see that famous ship three times again: once as a hospital ship, painted dazzling white with an emerald band and red crosses, in the Eastern Mediterranean during the Great War ; next, when I actually sailed on her from New York to Plymouth through five days and nights of a violent winter gale which she seemed to regard with a superb indifference ; and last of all on a lovely summer's evening on the Yorkshire coast, when with her lights ablaze, she steamed slowly north on her last voyage to the ship-breaker's yards at Rosyth. But my first view of her will always remain the most stirring of my memories of ships, and for the same reason perhaps, Liverpool, spiritual home of Cunard, stands first in my regard among the great seaports of England, even though the economics of Atlantic trade were to ordain the diversion of the fast passenger and mail service to Southampton.

It was the start of a day of mounting excitements and unbelievable joy. I was not bothered about my aunt and uncle. I did feel a bit sad when I thought of mother, and how she would have liked to have been in Liverpool again, but then I quickly thought that most likely she would have wanted to spend most of the time shopping. I wanted to see the docks and ships, and see them I did, or at least as much of them as I could in the course of that swiftly passing day. I could tell where the docks were by the smell of them, without the sight of masts and funnels rising above the roofs of warehouses ; a smell compounded of oil and smoke and tar and spices, a smell that lingers on a ship even when she is miles from land, and is accentuated rather than overcome by the briney vapours of the open sea. There were steamers, huge ones, so close to the dock walls that you could actually touch them. Some had English names. Others were foreign and they were flying foreign flags which I had never seen before. But there was no mistaking a Japanese ship, for there were Japanese sailors on her, and I could scarcely bring myself to move on to the next ship, they were so fascinating. There were Indians, too, wearing turbans ; and I saw a real Chinaman with a pigtail, although he had it coiled up under his hat, and there were dozens of negroes, although to my disappointment they wore ordinary sailors' clothes. I should have preferred to have seen them wearing animal skins, and carrying shields and spears !

I must have gone from ship to ship from dock to dock with my mouth wide open, and my eyes bulging with wonderment. What I could not understand was why Dad should ever have wanted to leave Liverpool and live in a little fishing village when there were so many exciting things to see. I actually saw one of the docks working, and a big steamer, with her decks piled up with new timber come in, straight from the Baltic ; I came to a graving dock, only it was about six times as big as the one at Whitby, and there was a steamer in it, quite dry so that you could even see its keel. And there were scores of men chipping the paint from

LIVERPOOL IN 1846: SEEN FROM UPPER TRANMERE, CHESHIRE

Coloured lithograph by J. McGahey

THE SOUTH P[

THE WEST PROSPECT OF HIS

Coloured e[

DOVER IN 1739

By courtesy of the Parker Gallery, London

DCKYARD AT CHATHAM, 1738
& N. Buck

WHITBY, YORKSHIRE
Oil painting by Richard Eurich, 1934

its bottom, while others were putting fresh paint on; and on the deck another group of men were putting red-hot rivets into a steel plate, making a terrific row. The cranes alone made up for all my years of waiting and yearning. There was a crane at our village railway station that was worked by hand, and it had printed on it, LOAD NOT TO EXCEED 2 TONS. These cranes, and there were dozens of them, worked by steam, and their load was marked, 10 TONS, and even 20 TONS! And the things that were coming out, or going into those ships! Great packages with foreign printing on them, casks, rolls of paper, timber, iron rails, bales of cotton and bundles of hides, machinery, and even live cattle. Hundreds of men as well as the sailors themselves were helping in this work. Most of them were very big, and they may have looked rough, and I certainly heard a lot of bad language, and some of them singing songs which I knew were not nice, but I was used to that from the sailors and fishermen at home, and in spite of what Uncle James had said, I did not see any of them drunk or brawling. They were all too busy.

I did not see all of Liverpool's docks. Even in those days there were more than twenty miles of quayside, not including Birkenhead. I did not see Birkenhead, except in the distance across the Mersey. I did not see what perhaps would have been the greatest thrill of all, the great shipbuilding and ship-repairing works of Cammel Laird. I went on and on, seeing and marvelling, long past dinner time into the afternoon. I must have walked miles. I got tired, and very, very hungry. Dad had given me a shilling when he had seen us off at the station. I had already spent threepence out of this for my tram fare. But I could not see any place where I could buy anything to eat. I began to feel a bit uneasy about my aunt and uncle. I wondered if, when I got back, they would be so cross with me they would not give me anything to eat, and would just pray instead. And then a wonderful thing happened. I came to another big steamer and the surprising thing about it was that it had three ammonites painted on its funnel, just the same as Whitby has for its coat of arms. As I was staring up at it I noticed an elderly man with a peak cap and double-breasted navy blue jacket leaning over the rails. He suddenly smiled at me, and then beckoned me to come aboard up the companion ladder. I thought I had never met anyone so kind-looking and jovial. He asked me what my name was and where I had come from, and when I told him the name of my village, he actually said in the broadest Yorkshire voice,

" Well, by Gum! Ah come from Whitby masen. This is a Whitby-owned ship!"

He was the captain. He took me all over his ship, down into the holds and the engine room, explaining everything, but also asking me plenty of questions, and I told him about my aunt and uncle, and how I'd run away from them, and he only laughed and did not seem cross. Then

13

we went into his cabin and he showed me a lot of curios that he had brought from foreign parts, including a wonderful model native canoe, which he said I could have. I was so excited that I scarcely noticed a man in a white coat, who came into the cabin and laid the table, until he said,

" Tea's served, sir ! "

It was the climax of my day's adventure. We had tea, with ham and boiled eggs, and plenty of cakes to follow. The captain did not bother to say a blessing either before or after. But when we had finished, he said, still not seeming cross, that he expected my aunt and uncle would be getting a bit anxious about me, and that I ought to go back to them, or they might think I had been kidnapped or murdered. We were a long way from where the trams for West Derby started, but as he had to go to the Pier Head himself on business, he would take me there on the Overhead Railway, and that would give me a fine view of the Docks. . . . . It was a fine view, but it was a very quick one, and it was the last I was to see of Liverpool's Docks for many years, for my aunt and uncle took good care that I did not escape again during the rest of my stay, but they prayed and read the Bible at me so much they must have forgotten all about the heathens abroad.

I

WE island dwellers are apt to take the excellence of our ports and harbours for granted. Britain, we were taught at school, owes its greatness to its equable climate (neither too hot nor too cold), to its rich deposits of coal, to the traditional skill and foresight of its ship-builders, and to the equal skill, foresight and audactiy of its mariners, who as merchantmen or in the navy, won for us and maintained a safe supremacy upon the seven seas, so that we could sell or barter the goods we made anywhere we liked. Providence not only gave us coal, but also a fair amount of ironstone, and placed both reasonably close to each other, so that the coal could be used for smelting the iron and making it into steel ; and coal and iron were placed near enough to our seaports where the steel could be used for the building of the ships which would take the surplus coal and steel to other countries, and exchange them for the raw materials, which were essential for our other coal-fed industries ; cotton, for example, which because of our " not too hot " climate, we cannot grow ourselves.

Looking at the industrial map of Britain, it does seem that we have been blessed. The great coal measures extend from the Northumberland and Durham coast through Yorkshire, Lancashire, and the Midlands to Wales, in an irregularly slanting band. A similar band slants across the narrow waist of Scotland from Fife to Ayrshire. In north-east England

THE SHIPWRECK
Oil painting by J. M. W. Turner, 1805

we have the great seaports and harbours of the Tyne, Wear and Tees. Close to the East Midlands is Hull, and to the West Midlands, Manchester and Liverpool. The great coal beds of South Wales are nearer still to the ports of the Severn estuary ; and in Scotland, Glasgow in the west and Leith in the east, are admirably situated, not so much in regard to the actual export of coal, but in relation to the numerous industries of which coal is the life-blood. All these seaports and harbours have undoubtedly contributed and are contributing, a vital part to our country's commercial and military greatness. They are a vital link in the bonds of good will and identical democratic purpose that tie the British Commonwealth and the other free, or once-free nations of the world. But the mistake so many of us make is in regarding them as a special gift of providence, like the coal itself. The truth is that with one or two exceptions Great Britain had no natural good harbours. What you see of them to-day is for the most part man-made.

What are the physical conditions that go to make an ideal natural harbour? First it must have a safe approach from the sea, clear of reefs and sandbanks, or heavy cross currents. Its entrance should be deep but fairly narrow, with a slant to the exterior coast line, so that incoming waves are diverted ; and inside it should at once widen to a deep water basin with plenty of room for vessels to turn, yet not so expansive that vessels while turning or at anchor are unprotected from winds. Preferably the basin should be hemmed in with hills or high land, but its shores should lend themselves to the building of wharves, jetties and docks, roads and railways. For a harbour to be situated on a river mouth or estuary has its advantages, but also grave disadvantages. The river itself may afford a means of communication for smaller craft like barges to the interior of the country. But when in flood it will be a nuisance, and at all times it will deposit silt, not only in the harbour, but outside in the form of sand banks. Even Falmouth which (with the purely naval harbour of Milford Haven) perhaps comes nearest to the physical ideal, required a break-water to protect its magnificent basin from the Channel winds and swell. Plymouth and its sister port of Devonport required a breakwater too ; and if Portsmouth and Southampton lie snug from southerly gales in the lee of the Isle of Wight, and have many other natural advantages, these fine ports—as they are to-day—are very much the product of the engineer's ingenuity.

London itself, still the world's greatest seaport, had most of the original odds against it, although it is likely that there would have been no London of importance but for the haven its river and estuary afforded the ships of the Roman and subsequent " colonists." Few of our seaports are so completely man-made as this. To start with, the outer sea approaches to the London estuary along the Kent and Essex coasts are sown with treacherous sandbanks which from earliest time have been the mariner's dread. The great tidal currents of the North Sea and English Channel sweep across the estuary mouth, and with the tidal and fresh water currents of the Thames itself, conspire to choke the deep water channels with precipitated sand or mud. And then, from Gravesend and Tilbury, where the Port of London may be said to begin, to London Bridge where it ends, the estuary writhes like a snake ; the whole of this passage from the open sea, a matter of fifty miles, is one that has always been subject to dense fogs and mists, and the Thames itself in full spate and with a spring tide, is by nature quite a turbulent river.

To me one of the most romantic and exciting aspects of our seaports is the making of them, a feat perhaps not so dramatic as the making of Sydney Bridge or the Great Boulder Dam, but one that has been in progress from the earliest days and can never cease while Britain maintains her place among the maritime nations of the world. Most of them began as mere fishing villages or settlements, and with primitive man the river mouth or estuary site would be a great advantage. All our rivers then would be as well-stocked with salmon as those of Alaska and Siberia and he would be able to make his choice of salt or fresh water fish. The river, too, would be an easy means of communication with the interior for bartering purposes ; dried fish for the corn or cattle of the purely rural or forest dweller, a trade which goes on to-day between the coast tribes and the interior tribes of many primitive countries. But the river mouth would also be the goal of the continental marauders and invaders ; these fishing villages equally obvious landing places. The villages might have been plundered and burnt, their inhabitants slaughtered, yet, as with the Romans and their plans for national conquest, the sites would have a strong strategic value, taking on now the importance of bridge-heads, and as their vessels were of heavier draught they would build jetties of sorts. Traces of such works have been found on the Thames bank in London, and at several other seaports.

In successive centuries with the consolidation of Britain as a nation, and her concern in offensive and defensive continental wars, her havens became of still greater strategic importance. Ships were vital to her existence. She built them from her native oak, the one-time fishing villages becoming ship yards as well as ports ; and because these were real ships, drawing a fair amount of water, substantial harbour works were necessary. But it was not until the Elizabethan Age, the age of commercial as well as naval and military expansion, that they began to take the shape of the ports as we know them to-day. Their story is tightly woven into the story of Britain's rise to greatness. London, Bristol, Plymouth, Falmouth were the chief ports of the Elizabethan adventurers. Then with the " discovery " of the commercial value of coal, the dawn of the great industrial age, came the rise of ports like Glasgow, Liverpool, Newcastle, Hull and Cardiff.

The steamship was a late comer into the industrial age. Long after the invention of the steam engine and the development of rail transport our growing export and import trade was being borne in wooden ships. That they were grand ships, manned by a grand breed of men, goes without saying ; yet how many of us realise what a perilous business this was, and what a debt we owe to these pioneers of our purely mercantile navy? Visit any of our great seaports to-day and you will see the most wonderful devices for the unloading and off-loading of ships, for moving them in and out of docks or alongside jetties. Channels are deep and accurately buoyed, and they extend well out to the open sea. Remember, too, that a steamship even in bad weather can move in any direction, astern if needs be, whereas a sailing ship can never go astern under her own power, and if she has a head-wind she must make a zigzag course. If our ports and harbours had been as they are to-day, navigating a sailing ship in or out of them would have been a difficult job. In the pioneer days, before the coming even of the steam tug, it must have called for very great skill on the part of officers and crew.

The Tyne, at Newcastle and Gateshead, when Queen Victoria came to the throne, was a narrow, turbulent river running between cliffs, and there was a bar at its mouth with only six feet of water at low tide. Here

again were fierce tides and a rock-bound coast subject to gales and sudden fogs. There were lighthouses then of sorts, but no mechanical sirens, and, of course, no radio or submarine fog-signalling devices. To make the Tyne, an incoming ship would have to wait for a favourable state of wind and tide, and God help her if, while waiting, she was caught by a northerly or easterly gale before there was enough water on the bar and she was unable to make an offing. They were necessarily small ships, the first of the Newcastle colliers, and many of them were built and owned at Whitby. Whitby then had two stone piers, shorter than they are to-day, but affording a safe haven in any weather once their entry was made. Here again, however, was a wicked bar, impassable at low water. On a day in October, 1861, a large number of Newcastle colliers, delayed by foul winds, were at anchor in Whitby Roads when, without warning, a fierce south-easterly gale sprang up. The tide was low so that the harbour was closed. Wind and sea, and the turning spring-tide current were soon too violent to permit any of the fleet to beat out to sea, and in the course of the storm which lasted two days and nights, nearly a score of them were driven on to the beach and smashed to bits. There would have been an appalling death roll but for the gallantry of the Whitby lifeboatmen who rescued the crews of twelve vessels before the lifeboat herself capsized with the loss of all her crew save one. Altogether nearly a hundred vessels were lost in that terrible storm at various places along the coast. Look in the old graveyards of the parish churches of any of

THE EDDYSTONE LIGHTHOUSE, *c.*1750
Engraving of Rudyard's wooden Lighthouse

our seaports and you will find a grim yet stirring commentary on the eighteenth and early nineteenth centuries' history of British shipping, which runs parallel with the history of her ports.   Here is a typical tombstone: 'TO THE LOVING MEMORY of William Moorsholm, Master Mariner of the brig *Fanny Dale* lost with all hands while on passage from Newcastle to London. . . . Also of his son, Thomas Moorsholm, Master Mariner, of the schooner *Excelsior*, sunk in collision off the mouth of the Thames. . . . Also of Richard and Henry Moorsholm, sons of the above and apprentices on the above schooner *Excelsior* when dire misfortune befell . . .'

Ironically the most dangerous hours of a voyage in the old days of sail were when a vessel was making for the very harbour where she would find refuge ; and thus safety was the prime consideration in the construction of our ports, a process which was stimulated by the coming of steam. For steamers, if they were independent of calms and foul winds, were just as liable to ground on inadequately marked reefs or sandbanks. They were equally helpless in fogs.   Besides, British trade was now expanding by leaps and bounds.   Steamships would be bigger than sailing ships, drawing more water even when in ballast.   New and more powerful lighthouses must be erected along our coasts, marking all danger points. Sandbanks must be carefully surveyed and conspicuously marked with buoys or light vessels.   Piers or sea walls must be built so that the entrances to harbours would be protected from the vagaries of the weather, and such things as bars must be removed. Coal was the mainspring of it all. But there was coal in other parts of the world. This natural treasure and even our merchant navy might have availed us nothing if it had not been for the spirit, the inventive genius and the industry of the engineers who, undeterred by the enormous problems that confronted them, laid the foundations of our ports and harbours as we know them to-day.

II

THE ports and harbours of Great Britain are not easily classified. In the old days it would have been simple, for most of them were granted charters called "staples," giving them the exclusive right to trade in specified products. You could say to-day that Newcastle and Cardiff are the chief coal ports and that Manchester and Liverpool stand for cotton, and Glasgow for shipbuilding, and Hull and Grimsby for fish, and Southampton for passenger traffic, and London for about everything except coal. Newcastle and Cardiff certainly are the country's chief coal ports, but it would be bad economy if a ship took a cargo of coal, say, from Cardiff to the Argentine, and came back empty for another one. The principles of barter apply to ports as they do to countries. The ship would return with a cargo of grain or hides or tallow to be discharged at Cardiff whose docks are equipped for handling general as well as specialised merchandise. Liverpool and Manchester may have a virtual "staple" in the import of raw and the export of manufactured cotton; but despite the divergence of the fastest Atlantic passenger traffic to Southampton, Liverpool remains among the world's premier passenger ports, and she and Manchester have a huge share in the handling of general merchandise as imports and exports.

Although rather outside the scope of our title, this survey would be incomplete without a passing reference to Ireland and the great city and seaport of Belfast, which is situated at the head of Belfast Lough. The approaches to the harbour are safe and easy and it has a fine system of docks and the fact that all the coal used has to be imported has in no way retarded its development. The chief industry there is shipbuilding and the great firm of Harland and Woolf alone employed over 25,000 men even before the present war; but Belfast is also an important manufacturing town whose main industries are linen weaving, distilling and rope-making.

The truth is that all our great seaports have a general as well as a specialised trade. Glasgow and Newcastle build ships, but they import grain and fruit and timber. Hull and Grimsby are best known as fishing ports, but in peace time they have an immense trade in timber with Scandinavia and Russia. Hull (again in peace time) competes with Newcastle and Leith in the passenger and fresh fruit traffic to the

ROSYTH DOCKYARD : AFTERNOON
Drawing by Sir Muirhead Bone

countries of Northern Europe, yet both trade direct with America, North and South, the Far East and the countries of the British Commonwealth.

Let us then make a broad survey of the coasts of Great Britain, starting at the north-east tip of Scotland and coming south. In this part of Scotland there are no deposits of coal or other important minerals. Even agriculture is confined to a comparatively narrow belt between the coast and the bleak mountainous interior. In a stretch of more than a hundred miles, until we get to Inverness, Wick is the only seaport marked in conspicuous type on the map, although there is the important naval base of Invergordon on the Cromarty Firth, and from Inverness east to Rattray Head, then south to Aberdeen, there are only Lossiemouth, Fraserburgh, and Peterhead. Wick and the last three may indeed be said to have a " staple " trade in fish. That wide triangle of sea enclosed by a line drawn from Duncansby Head to Rattray Head, with its apex the Moray Firth, is famous as a herring ground. It is here that the herring fleets, English as well as Scotch, start fishing in early spring gradually following the shoals south through summer and early autumn to East Anglia. But even as fishing ports Wick, Lossiemouth, Fraserburgh are small and seasonal in their activities. The picturesque city and seaport of Inverness owes its comparative importance to its situation at the head

ENTRANCE TO THE PORT OF DUNDEE
Engraving from Finden's *Ports, Harbours and Watering Places,* 1839

of the Caledonian Canal. But the canal does not tap any vast industrial area and Aberdeen, although a seaport and city of size, has had its industrial development limited by the absence of nearby coal. Aberdeen's chief industry is, of course, fishing, not so much herring as deep-sea trawling, the annual value of her landings reaching well over the value of two million pounds in normal times. Aberdeen has a good harbour, and many general industries including granite quarrying, brewing and distilling, paper-making, and the manufacture of textiles. But all her coal must be imported from the south, and her chief shipping trade, apart from fish, is coastal. Moving south from Aberdeen there are the minor fishing ports of Stonehaven, Montrose and Arbroath : then, on the Firth of Tay, nearer to the coal beds of Fifeshire we get one of Scotland's most important seaports, Dundee, with its jute and linen mills and other extensive industries, including brewing and distilling, and jam-making, all or nearly all dependent on coal for power and on foreign ship-borne cargoes for their raw material. Dundee's principal import is raw jute, shipped direct from India. The county of Fife, rich in coal and iron, may be considered as a wide peninsula, between the Firth of Tay and the Firth of Forth. It forms the eastern boundary of Scotland's industrial and agricultural lowland belt which reaches west to Glasgow. The Firth of Forth apart from its importance as a naval haven—with Rosyth as

22

NEWCASTLE-UPON-TYNE
Engraving from Finden's *Ports, Harbours and Watering Places*, 1840

harbour and base—forms a sort of eastern equivalent of the Clyde, and the port of Leith, which adjoins the city of Edinburgh, more than rivals Dundee as an all-round seaport and industrial town. It has a fine artificial harbour, excellent docks and vast warehouses, and like Dundee scores over Glasgow in its nearness to the Continent with which, in peace time, the bulk of its trade is carried on. Indeed most of Glasgow's own trade with the Continent passes through Leith via the railway system and the Clyde Canal which connects the two ports.

On the south side of the Forth is Grangemouth, with a large continental and coastwise trade, and imports of timber and iron ore. A good deal of the latter goes to the famous Carron iron works three miles from Grangemouth where most of Wellington's cannon were made.

Also on the south side are the smaller ports of Bo'ness, Granton and Newhaven (engaged chiefly in deep-sea fishing) and on the north side, Largo (port of Alexander Selkirk), and the coal ports of Burtisland and Methil.

Rosyth is one of Britain's finest naval bases with splendid dock yards and facilities for repairing and maintaining our biggest battleships ; it was Beatty's cruiser base in the last war. It was in the Firth of Forth that the German Navy surrendered to Beatty, sailing in through twenty-three miles of British and American warships !

As we move south across the border it becomes increasingly evident that the size and importance of our seaports is related directly to coal ; not so much to coal as a prime export, but as the raw material of other industries. Coal and industry determine the density of population. They increase it physically and economically at the expense of agriculture, the direct producer of food. It is not that factories and cities actually occupy land that once grew corn and potatoes. The total land covered by a city like Sheffield, for example, is relatively insignificant. But industry, with its higher wages, saps the man power of agriculture. It makes goods in excess of its own capacity for consumption. It must trade these with other countries, which obviously must produce something else, and as this something is mostly the product of agriculture the home-grown product must be reduced. It is a vicious circle which perhaps will never be broken except by international goodwill and co-operation. The fact remains that where you get coal you get industry, and a density of population that must be fed chiefly with imported foods which must be transported and unloaded and distributed swiftly through ports. There is no coal between the Lothians and Northumberland ; there are no big industrial areas ; there are no seaports of size until we get to the Tyne, where we have Shields and Newcastle.

The Tyne still spells coal, although its export trade suffered a severe set-back in the slump that followed the boom years of the last war when many continental markets were lost for ever. As world trade began to recover slowly from its sickness a new factor arose which was to prove a serious menace to the coal export industry. This was the use of oil as fuel, not only in ships but in overseas industries which hitherto had depended entirely on coal imported from this country. Had the Tyne herself been dependent exclusively on the export of coal for her prosperity it is likely that the onset of the present war would have found the people of North and South Shields, Jarrow, Gateshead and Newcastle in complete distress. Things were not too good, it is true ; but shipbuilding, the river's chief creative industry, was well on the up-grade then, although, ironically enough, most of the ships being built were oil-burning and even oil-carrying !

I made a tour of north-east industrial England during the winter of 1935 when the Tyne was classified as a " distressed area." The shipyards at Jarrow had been permanently closed under a scheme which had for its object the rationalisation of the shipbuilding industry as a whole. Thousands of skilled men had been unemployed and on the dole for months on end. It was pitiful to see these men standing outside the employment exchanges. They were not starved. The " dole " at least gave them food. They were not ill-clad or dirty. In fact, their cleanliness and the whiteness of their hands were as tragically significant as the expression of boredom and hopelessness in their eyes. There were at that time scores of merchant

IRON AND COAL : THE INDUSTRY OF THE TYNE
Water colour by W. B. Scott, 1811-1890

steamers " laid-up " in the river, with only a watchman on board, their crews and officers all unemployed. I visited the vast ship yards of Swan Hunter's and was shown the very slip on which the *Mauretania* had been built. In the whole yard, there was only one ship on the stocks, a small destroyer which, I think, was being built for a foreign country. Most of the coal staiths whose mechanical equipment of hoists and conveyors is the finest in the world were idle and it was the same at Sunderland and Hartlepool and Middlesbrough where all but one of the numerous blast furnaces were cold, and there were not more than three ships in port, and these foreign. But I was fortunate to repeat my visit to the North-East at a later period when, with the stimulus of the Government subsidy to tramp-shipping and the general improvement in world trade, things were moving back to normal.

It was not a boom. It needed a war to produce that. There were plenty of men, young and old, loafing round the employment exchanges,

25

but all the shipyards were working to at least half their capacity, and orders were coming in fast. There was an exhilarating optimism in the air. An industrial depression is a vicious circle. A slack period in a town's chief industry affects not only its auxiliary trade (with shipbuilding, for example, the wire and cable, ship-furnishing, paint and varnish and electric fittings trades) but the retail shops, public services like trams, gas and electricity, and places of amusement. Only the pawnshop prospers. Thanks to subsidies, and subtle political machinations, certain foreign states had been able to make a serious challenge to Britain's long-maintained supremacy in ocean transport. But British shipowners saw that it required more than a subsidy to beat this competition. The days of the old slow tramp had gone. New ships were required, economy ships they were called. Oil bunkers took up less space in a ship than coal. Oil took less time to load, making for a quicker turnabout in port. Speed, not only at sea, but in loading and discharging cargoes was everything. Hulls were being streamlined to take every advantage of increased power : and (in one sense unfortunately for the personnel of the merchant navy) these ships were labour-saving and therefore required a smaller crew. Most of the ships I saw under construction on this visit had an impressive beauty of shape, with their clipper bows and cutaway stern, and raked funnels. They were not all general-cargo ships. There were tankers and ore carriers, and fruit and meat ships. There were warships, too ; and as activity in a chief trade reverses the vicious circle caused by depression, there was more business in the shops and cinemas, above all at the football grounds on Saturday afternoons. Even at Jarrow, the most hard-hit of the Tyne ports, things were better. There was no shipbuilding, but a revived ship-breaking industry had absorbed a fair number of the local unemployed, and there was a promise of new industries being started. The ship-repairing industry of the Tyne was also in full swing again. Here some incredible feats of naval engineering were being carried out, notably the fitting of new bows and a new stern onto an old tramp steamer, thereby increasing her length and cargo-carrying capacity to be in line with her new oil-burning engines !

The north-east industrial area extends south to the Tees, and includes the ports of Sunderland and Hartlepool. Both are concerned primarily with coal and shipbuilding and marine engineering, and their chief imports are timber from the Baltic, principally pit-props for the Durham coal mines. They both have fine artificial harbours, accessible at any state of tide and weather to the largest cargo vessels, with ample wet and dry dock capacity. With those of the Tyne, their yards and marine engineering works have a higher shipbuilding potential than any similarly associated group in the world. And it is to the lasting credit of the shipbuilding masters and men that they courageously weathered those terrible

STAITHES, YORKSHIRE
Oil painting by Richard Eurich

post-war years of depression and that the industry was on its toes to meet
the challenge of another and greater war. Hartlepool, by the way (like
Shields at the mouth of the Tyne) is also a deep-sea fishing port, with a
seasonal trade in herrings.

The river Tees forms the south boundary of the Durham coal field.
It also marks the northern limit of the Cleveland ironstone deposits,
and it was to the conjunction of these two minerals that the city and port
of Middlesbrough owes its existence. It was not until 1830 that its
first house was built, and like the Tyne, the Tees itself was almost
unnavigable. To-day, with the practically adjoining towns of Thornaby
and Stockton it is the centre of a great iron and steel-producing district.
Here are blast furnaces which in normal times of prosperity darken the
daylight sky, and at night redden it and afford a sure beacon to the
incoming mariner, long before he has sighted the red and white flash
of the South Gare lighthouse at the river mouth. Here, too, are the roll-
ing mills and forges that made the girders of Sydney Bridge, the bridge
over the Zambesi near the Victoria Falls, and many other famous con-
structions in all parts of the world. Here hundreds of thousands of ships'

plates and castings are made, yet, curiously enough, there are few big shipbuilding yards on the Tees. The port of Middlesbrough exists chiefly for the export of pig-iron, steel rails and girders, the raw material of the constructional engineer ; and, more curiously, her chief import is iron ore, for the ironstone of the Cleveland Hills requires a mixture of other special grades to make the steel for which her furnaces and mills are renowned. But the port has also a big general trade and (again in peace time) you will find in it many foreign ships from Europe, America and, particularly, Japan.

From the Tees south to the Humber we have a coalless and exclusively agricultural near-interior. It is a shallow and, as far as Flamborough Head, a rocky coast, with only one small river, the Esk, and few natural havens. Whitby, Scarborough and Bridlington are the only harbours and all three are tidal and inaccessible at low water for all except small fishing craft. Between these are the picturesque and once prosperous fishing villages of Staithes (the " Steers " of Laura Knight's fascinating auto-biography) Runswick, Robin Hood's Bay (the " Bramblewick " of my own novels) Filey and Flamborough. It was the steam trawler that caused their economic decay. Men fishing in small open pulling and sailing cobles, dependent always on the vagaries of the weather, and restricted to close-in grounds could not possibly compete against ships which in any weather could catch more fish and fetch it to port and market with unfail-ing regularity. Most of the young men of these villages either emigrated to the trawling ports like North Shields, Hartlepool, Hull or Grimsby, or joined the mercantile marine. But with the development of the internal combustion engine there was a revival in semi-inshore fishing after the last war. The open coble had gone of course ; what made the revival possible was the Scotch-built " keeler," a sturdy craft, equipped with a diesel engine capable of a speed of eight knots and of standing up to any sort of weather. They have a comparatively big draught, so that they were no good for the harbourless villages. But they were just right for Whitby, Scarborough and Bridlington where, up to the outbreak of the present war, there were substantial fleets, which if they did not offer a serious competition to the steam trawler, benefited in the market by the fact that their catch was fresher ; also, that in the seasonal glut of " round " fish, the " keelers " could switch over to crab and lobster fishing in which there was no competition at all. Trawlers and "keelers" and herring drifters and their men, have alike been affected by the war. The majority of boats and men are now engaged on fishing for a more elusive and perilous quarry than fish.

HULL : VIEW OF THE TOWN FROM THE RIVER
Etching by W. Hollar, 1640

III

COMPARED with the heavily industrialised and densely populated areas of which the Tyne, Wear and Tees ports are the centre, it would seem at a first glance that Hull is the centre of an agricultural area, and that the argument that the size of seaports is related to the nearness of coal must fail. Hull is certainly not situated on a coal bed. Neither is there any great industrial area close by. But it happens that she lies on an estuary which with its rivers and their tributaries and canals connects her, not only with the coal beds of West Yorkshire and their vast associated industries, but with the chief industrial towns of Lancashire, the Midlands, even with London. Water transport is slower but cheaper than rail. Barges can carry loads of 150 tons between Hull and Leeds, for example, and these may be loaded by what is called " overside dis- charge," that is, direct from ship's hold to barge, thus saving dock and warehouse charges. Altogether Hull is the base for six hundred miles of inland water navigation ; and, because of her nearness to the big conti- nental ports, it is not surprising that she handles much of the normal continental export and import trade through her spacious and well- equipped docks. Her trade is not confined to the Continent, however. She is the natural raw material port for the wool industry of West York- shire. She handles immense quantities of grain and oil-bearing seed to supply her own flour and oil-cake mills. She exports coal and imports coal-mine timber. She is a fishing port too, with a fleet of two hundred and fifty steam trawlers, probably the biggest of any single port in the world, and with an annual catch worth almost four million pounds. As a by-product she produces meal and fertilisers from fish offal (once thrown overboard) and cod and halibut oil ; and there are smoke-curing factories.

Hull is not the only Humber port. Goole, higher up the estuary, is nearer to the coalfields and the inland waterways, and in many respects is a miniature Hull without a fishing industry, although she shares in this by building fishing craft. Grimsby almost at the estuary mouth is still

GRIMSBY : SELLING FISH
Water colour by Thomas Rowlandson, 1756-1827

the best-known deep-sea fishing port in Great Britain in spite of Hull's claim to a bigger fleet. A friendly rivalry exists between them, but whichever way the balance of fleet or catch goes it is certainly a small one. Both ports maintain a North Sea and an Iceland fleet. The ships of the former are mostly small and a trip usually lasts about a week. The " Iceland " ships are much larger, very fast, and are equipped with baths and very comfortable accommodation for their crews. They have refrigerating apparatus, so that their catch suffers little from the longer time at sea, and at both ports the facilities for discharging it, selling it, and despatching it to inland towns are admirable. One should visit the fish docks at Hull or Grimsby at six o'clock on a winter's morning to get a true impression of this phase in the epic of a sole, which starts way out on the North Sea, and ends as a Sole Meunière in an elegant London restaurant—or of an Iceland cod, sold in batter-plastered sections with a penn'orth of chips in a fried fish shop in Wigan.

The trawlers, their rigging festooned with icicles and frozen spray, their decks maybe inches deep in snow and slush, are berthed end to end along the walls of the fish dock, close up to the immense continuous shed which forms the market and contains centrally, the offices of the buyers. In peace time the decks of the trawlers are illuminated with powerful flood lights. The fish-holds are open. Screeching derricks hoist the fish up in boxes, baskets, or singly if they happen to be giant Iceland or

A FISHMARKET ON THE BEACH
Water colour by Thomas Rowlandson, 1756-1827

White Sea halibut or skate. They are swung round on to chutes, that slant straight into the shed, where gangs of sea-booted, oil-skinned men seize them and lay them out on the spotlessly clean concrete floor of the shed. When discharging is complete the auctioneers ring their bells. The buyers gather round, and by a seemingly unintelligible combination of rapid-fire speech, head-nod and other sign-language, the fish are sold, and the buyers' men haul them away to be washed, packed, consigned and loaded into special trucks of the fish trains (bound for various inland towns) that are waiting at the opposite side of the shed. Usually by half-past eight you will not see a sign of a fish in the entire market. The trawlers have moved on to another wharf where they are taking in bunkers, fresh water, ice, and stores again ready for another voyage. Grimsby has commercial as well as fishing docks and handles a good proportion of the continental trade, especially timber. Five miles up the Humber is the purely commercial dock of Immingham, built and still owned by one of the great railway companies.

South from Grimsby we find another long stretch of coast without towns or harbours of great importance. Lincolnshire is an agricultural county with no coal and the coast is flat, regular and shallow. There are, how-ever, two small ports in the Wash of great historical interest, Boston and King's Lynn. Both lie at the start of canal systems, leading through a predominantly agricultural country into the industrial Midlands. They

31

are handicapped by the shallowness of their sea approaches, but they are important links in the purely coastal trade of Great Britain, and Boston, too, has a fishing industry. Norfolk, Suffolk and Essex again are agricultural counties, very flat, with no big industrial areas except in the south of Essex, and with a regular shallow coast that is fringed with sand banks. There are abundant rivers, but they are mostly shallow and only fitted for barge traffic. Yarmouth and Lowestoft, the only seaports between the Wash and Harwich owe their fame to the fact that they lie close to the seasonal migratory route of the herring shoals, and that the entire herring fleet of the British Isles (and also many continental fishing craft) are based here during summer and autumn. At this time both ports are the scene of prodigious activity. Speed is more important with herring than with any other sort of fish for they deteriorate under any direct economical process of refrigeration. They are caught close in to the coast within the short hours of the summer and autumn nights, and the drifters make for port at top speed as soon as their nets are hauled. Off-loading starts the very moment they are berthed. The fish are auctioned, but at Yarmouth and Lowestoft only a proportion are packed and despatched as fresh herrings for home consumption. The local curers buy most of the catch. Some are pickled. For this process hundreds of girls make an annual migration to East Anglia from the Western Highlands of Scotland and the Orkneys. These girls speak Gaelic and are famous for their good looks, and offer a perennial subject for the press photographer. They gut the herrings with incredible speed and dexterity, throw them into huge wooden troughs containing salt, then pack them into barrels which (again in normal times) are shipped to the Continent, especially Russia. But for home consumption herrings are cured into kippers or bloaters, or canned. Yarmouth has huge factories for this industry capable of producing millions of kippers and bloaters in a season.

As we move south to the Essex coast we are approaching the mighty industrial area of which London is the heart, and at the same time coming nearer to the continental seaboard. Harwich is the first of several ports which are engaged principally with express passenger and goods traffic across the Channel. The town itself is very old and its harbour and fortifications were important enough to be attacked by Dutch naval forces in 1666. This harbour has been modernised, and in 1924 was equipped as a train ferry station enabling passengers (and express goods) to travel from London to Zeebruge and the continental railway systems without change from rail to ship and from ship to train again.

ENTRANCE TO PORTSMOUTH HARBOUR

Oil painting by J. Lynn, 1846

FALMOUTH HARBOUR, C.1840

Coloured lithograph by Newman & Co.

IV

LEAVING London until the end of this survey, let us cross the mouth of the Thames estuary to the coast of Kent. Here at last is coal again, but its exploitation is only recent, and both in quality and quantity is of comparative unimportance. From here, however, and along the whole of the south coast as far as Southampton, the chief economic factors that have directed the rise and development of the coastal towns and ports have been the influence of London as the political and commercial capital, and the immense population of the city, outer London and her satelite towns: these and the proximity of the continental seaboard. Thus Chatham with Rochester and Sheerness may be regarded as London's naval base and dockyard and the stronghold of her fortifications: Margate, Ramsgate, Hythe, Hastings, Brighton as her seaside resorts: Dover, Folkestone, Newhaven as her continental ferry ports. Apart from that in Kent, there is no coal in the south of England: but it is the heavy industries like iron and steel smelting, shipbuilding, and the concentrated ones like cotton and wool, and motor cars, that are so dependent on a near supply of coal. The industries of the south are "light" and diverse, and, after all, they are not so very far away by rail and road and sea from the coal of South Wales and the Midlands. And again the energy of coal is brought to them, in the most convenient form of all for "light" industries, along the cables of the electric grid.

In the old days, London, great though she was herself, had what might be called her satelite seaports. There were five of them and they were known as the Cinque ports: Dover, Sandwich, Hastings, Romney and Hythe, although later Winchelsea and Rye were added to their number. Their chief duty was to furnish ships to the State. In the reign of Edward I they had to provide fifty-seven ships for a period of fifteen days without direct recompense, but they had many privileges, such as an exemption from taxes. Of the Cinque ports, only Dover to-day remains commercially significant, and Rye and Winchelsea have ceased to be ports, owing to the silting up of their harbours. Indeed, the whole of the south coast from Folkestone to the Isle of Wight has no big seaport. The main industrial artery of which London is the heart runs direct to Southampton, which challenges Liverpool's claim to be the second port of the Kingdom.

Southampton, although her origins are ancient, is of comparatively recent development. In fact, her first dock was not built until a hundred years ago. Before that, of course, the artery with London did not exist, nor were there any life-lines with the Midlands. She had no industries of her own save wooden shipbuilding. The natural advantages of her harbour and position were to become obvious enough in the dawn of the industrial age. She was near the Continent; she had an advantage over London in that ocean-going ships had a shorter and safer route up and down the Channel ; her position was very sheltered ; she had the unique advantage of four high tides in the twenty-four hours, a phenomenon produced by the peculiar position of the Isle of Wight, and with the average fall between high and low water very small. Her close approaches were shallow, but the bottom was soft, and with the invention of the bucket steam-dredger Southampton Water became a deep channel, that became deeper still as the port developed and ships became bigger, until to-day the two biggest vessels afloat, *Queen Mary* and *Queen Elizabeth* could steam in perfect safety up and down the fairway. Not only this, they could go alongside the quays of the Ocean Dock without entering through locks and disembark their passengers direct into railway expresses for London and all parts of England. Again, for repairs or re-fitting these giant liners could enter the George V graving dock and dry out with greater ease and safety than one of the old Whitby brigs could enter the Whitehall dry dock.

No wonder that Southampton stole the express Transatlantic passenger service from Liverpool ; and her importance is not confined to this. A passenger sailing-list for May, 1939 includes, apart from the crack Atlantic liners of Great Britain, France, Germany and Holland, such names as the *Arandora Star*, *Arundel* and *Dunbar Castle*, and sailings to and arrivals from Australia, Japan, India, Egypt, South America, Jamaica, West, South and East Africa. And the passenger traffic represents only one side of the port's shipping activities. She has an immense import trade in fruit, grain, frozen meat, timber, wool and hides, and mineral oil. She exports the manufactures of South and Midland England. Because of her central position and closeness to the Continent, she has a large re-export trade too, re-shipping goods, for instance, from America to Turkey or from Belgium to South Africa, or the Plate to Denmark. In many ways Southampton is the most compact and up-to-date port in Great Britain, with thriving industries of her own, which include shipbuilding and aircraft-production, and is herself an airport, the base of the Empire Service of flying boats which still maintain communication with Egypt, South Africa, India and Australia.

Of the purely naval port of Portsmouth (" Pompey " as she is known in the Service) we shall have nothing to say beyond that she has a fine harbour, with dockyards, engineering works and arsenals which, since the days of Nelson, have made an immeasurable contribution to Great Britain's strength. Between Portsmouth and Southampton, on the opposite side of the Solent, is the seaport of Cowes which, if very small, is world famous as the headquarters of the Royal Yacht Squadron and for its annual regatta. On a fine summer's day before the war, the Solent might have offered to the spectator standing on the chalk hills above Cowes, a picture symbolic of Great Britain's everlasting concern with the sea :

SOUTHAMPTON
The *Majestic* in the King George V graving dock

the pale blue Solent speckled with the white sails of racing and pleasure yachts and the barked sails of fishing craft ; ferry boats plying to and from Southampton and Portsmouth and the Isle of Wight ; small coastal steamers ; cross Channel packets bound for (or from) the Channel Islands, Cherbourg or St. Malo ; Cardiff colliers ; ocean-going tramps ; long, sleek tankers bringing oil from Mexico or the Dutch East Indies, or molasses from the Windward Isles ; banana and citrus fruit ships ; crack motor liners inward or outward bound for India, the Cape, Australia or South America, some engaged on what had then become one of the most popular types of summer holiday for the moderately well-to-do, the pleasure cruise : Atlantic liners, perhaps the *Europa* or the *Normandie*, the newly built *Mauretania* the second, or mighty *Queen Mary* herself : destroyers too, grey, sombre and rather sinister : cruisers ; maybe a whole naval squadron steaming out from Portsmouth for exercises, with battleships and an aircraft carrier, with scores of fighter and reconnaisance planes circling above ; and perhaps in serene contrast a huge Empire flying boat, inward bound from Australia gliding down to its journey's end.

There is no coal along the south coast of England and as one goes west from Southampton the heart-pumps of industrial and densely populated London weaken in their inward and outward thrusts which draw in food and raw material from the seven seas and force out manufactures. Weymouth in Dorsetshire has a good harbour and an export trade chiefly with London in the famous Portland stone which is quarried here. She is a packet port too for the Channel Islands, but she is better known as a health resort and holiday centre. In fact, the whole coast from here to Devon and Cornwall is known as the English Riviera, with Torquay the modest and, of course, non-gambling equivalent of Monte Carlo. Even Plymouth—scene of that historic game of bowls played by Drake before he set out to trounce the ships of the Spanish Armada; home base of Raleigh, Gilbert, Grenville and many other Elizabethan sailors, fighters and explorers; port of departure for the *Mayflower* and the Pilgrim Fathers—is a popular holiday resort in peace time. There are no furnaces and very few factories to pollute the air or mask the loveliness of her Sound and its fringing cliffs, and the surrounding country, which rises in waves of low, rounded red-earthed hills to the dark massif of Dartmoor. Yet, with Devonport, Plymouth ranks second only to Portsmouth as a naval base and dockyard. She has very little export trade, but is an ocean passenger port, and some of the crack Atlantic liners, especially those bound direct for continental ports, call here to disembark passengers and British mail. In addition, Plymouth is the chief steam-trawling port of the south coast and a centre for the pilchard fishing and curing industry.

As we move west we are getting farther away from coal and industry. Cornwall once famous for its tin mines, has only one mineral of commercial importance. This is china clay, or kaolin, a substance resulting from the geological decomposition of her native granite. It is used, not only for the manufacture of pottery, but in the making of certain kinds of high-grade paper and paints, and is exported chiefly to Italy and the United States from Falmouth and Fowey, which was once famous as the base of the West India sailing packets. Cornwall's major industries are agriculture and fishing. Apart from Fowey and Falmouth, there are no harbours capable of floating vessels of any size, although there are scores of little harbours like Looe, Mevagissey, Coverack, Portleven, Penzance, and, on the north coast, St. Ives, Newquay, Padstow, Port Isaac, Bude. Some, like Looe and Penzance, can accommodate small coastal steamers, and Penzance has a regular import trade with the Scilly Isles in early vege-

TORQUAY FROM THE PAIGNTON ROAD
Water colour by a late eighteenth-century English artist

36

THE HOE, PLYMOUTH
Water colour by J. M. W. Turner, 1775-1851

tables and flowers. But they are all principally fishing ports and some are holiday resorts of inland townspeople. Many of them, unfortunately, have had their natural beauty marred by the building of hotels and boarding houses, and villas ; even promenades and concert pavilions. The real beauty of the original Cornish fishing village with its white-washed cottages, slate roofs and winding streets, is not the quaintness of them, but that they were built honestly by simple honest people out of native material without any pretensions to " art." The cottages had to be close to the harbour, and therefore close to each other. There were no motor cars then and no traffic problems, so that the streets climbed and twisted according to the site. Perhaps the least spoilt and loveliest of them all is Polperro, and this, I think, is because, in spite of economic adversity, her native population has persisted in fishing, and stolidly refused to be ousted by the summer hotel, or lodging-house keeper or caterer.

Falmouth is the best proof of all that the growth and prosperity of a seaport is related less to the physical advantages of its harbour than to the proximity of coal and industry. Falmouth harbour clearly merits the term magnificent. It is naturally deep and wide and, since the building of a long sea wall, is protected from all winds and is very easy of approach.

DARTMOUTH
Engraving from Stanfield's *Coast Scenery*, 1836

It was prosperous enough in sailing-ship days ; under adverse weather conditions an inward bound barque might make Falmouth three weeks before London and it was a very close rival to Bristol in ocean trade. But Bristol had coal on her doorstep, and although Falmouth owns splendid wet and dry docks, her activities as a seaport are chiefly confined to ship-repairing, although her exports of China clay were increasing up to the outbreak of the present war.

Bristol is one of the oldest seaports. It is recorded that as far back as the year A.D. 1000 she had a brisk export trade with Ireland in slaves ! In 1353 she was recognised as a staple port in wool, leather, wine and salt, and she played a big part in the discovery, colonisation and marine enterprise of the Elizabethan Age : Cabot sailed from Bristol in 1497. Her trade boomed in the early days of the Industrial Age. She was the natural outlet to the Atlantic for the manufactures of the south Midlands and attracted the main flow of American imports, especially sugar and tobacco. But as ships grew bigger her own approaches became inadequate and the rapidly developing port of Liverpool stole much of her import and export trade. Cardiff, which once had thrived by systematic piratage of Bristol's shipping began to steal her coal trade. But the building of a fine new system of docks at the mouth of the River Avon brought back much of Bristol's prosperity and while she is behind Southampton and

38

Liverpool in dock facilities for very large vessels she has a big share in the general Atlantic and Empire trade and has extensive light manufactures of her own, notably tobacco and cocoa. Cardiff, however, had won a supremacy in the export coal trade which she never surrendered. Not only was she situated close to inexhaustible deposits of coal, but to some of the richest anthracite beds in the world. Anthracite, being virtually smokeless, was the ideal fuel for warships until the coming of oil and for general commercial and domestic purposes it is doubtful whether it will ever be supplanted by any other fuel. Cardiff's docks were designed and built specially for the loading of coal, and their mechanical equipment of hoists and conveyors enables the biggest ships to load and turn about in an incredibly short space of time. But as I have said it would be bad economy if those ships came in empty, and the port is also engaged in an import trade of general merchandise, and it was this fact which helped Cardiff and her neighbouring ports of Newport and Swansea to weather the years of depression when the foreign export of coal dropped almost to zero. Again, these ports have their own industries : steel-making and shipbuilding and general engineering, although not so extensive as those of the Tyne.

RAMSGATE
Coloured aquatint from P. J. de Loutherbourg's
Romantic and Picturesque Scenery, 1805

V

MILFORD HAVEN near the most westerly tip of the coast of South Wales, and at the mouth of the Bristol Channel is probably the finest natural harbour in the British Isles, and it cannot be argued that in this case its failures to develop into a first-class commercial port is due to its remoteness from coal, for some of the richest beds are quite near. The explanation is that the navy got in first, built docks at Pembroke, and then, when the need for national economy became so acute after the last war, closed these docks down, a decision which even then caused some heartburnings among the experts on national security. Yet while there is coal in Pembrokeshire, its natural flow is to Swansea, and from Pembrokeshire north along the west coast of Wales the country is agricultural. There are no big industrial towns or seaports, although there are plenty of minor ones such as Cardigan and Aberayron, Barmouth, and Pwllheli with tidal harbours and a coastal trade, and, of course, there are the Irish packet ports of Fishguard in Pembroke and Holyhead in Anglesey. But with West Wales it may be that her mountainous interior is as much the cause of her lack of big seaports, as the direct absence of coal. It makes a barrier between the coast and the industrial Midlands. There are plenty of rivers, but they are short and turbulent, and there are no canals. And for an opposite reason, because there is a gap between the mountains of North Wales and the Pennines, and a plain in which the Mersey and its tributaries flow gently from the heart of an interior rich in coal, Liverpool is the biggest sea port and city on the west side of the British Isles.

Purely as a harbour site, Liverpool originally did not possess one fraction of the natural advantages of Milford Haven, Falmouth or Pembroke. The seaward approaches of the Mersey are exposed, and as thick with shifting sandbanks as the mouth of the Thames. The estuary was shallow and the surrounding country flat and marshy. It was cotton that gave the first big impetus to her development—not because she manufactured this herself, but because she was the natural port for Manchester, which on account of the humid conditions prevailing in that more inland district of Lancashire and the abundance of coal, had become the world's chief cotton city. Liverpool imported raw cotton from America, and sent it (first by rail) to Manchester, and she exported it again in the form of woven fabric back to America, and to every other corner of the world. But if her approaches and estuaries were dredged and her docks built principally for cotton, her position on the Atlantic seaboard drew other import and export trades, notably grain, timber, oils and fats and she was established as the premier Atlantic passenger port in the hey-day of American emigration and settlement. The building of the Manchester ship canal which made Manchester into a port

BRISTOL

Water colour by J. B. Pyne, 1800-1870

GREENOCK IN 1840

LEITH HARBOUR IN 1842
Coloured engravings from the drawings by W. H. Bartlett

naturally short-circuited a proportion of Liverpool's cargo shipping ; but this was offset by the general impetus it gave to the cotton and allied trades.

This canal was designed by Sir E. Leader Williams in 1882, but owing to political opposition it was not until 1885 that the Bill authorising its construction was passed by Parliament and another two years passed before work was begun. It was opened seven years later by Queen Victoria. It was an immense feat of engineering, for its purpose was to make Manchester accessible to ocean-going ships, which meant that it had to be considerably deeper and wider than the ordinary barge canal. Not only this, but there must be room for vessels to pass each other, or the traffic would be only one-way !

The total length is $35\frac{1}{2}$ miles. It begins at Eastham on the Cheshire side of the Mersey, and more or less follows the course of the Mersey estuary to Runcorn ; then goes inland near to Warrington, where tidal action ceases and it is fed by the waters of the River Mersey and the Irwell. There are three entrance locks which keep the water-level approximately that of mean tidal high water. At Barton the Bridgewater Canal actually crosses the ship canal on a swing aqueduct, and many railway lines cross it by high-level viaducts. Again at one point the River Gowy is taken underneath the Canal by means of huge syphons. Its cost was tremendous, but its benefit to Lancashire trade has been immeasurably great. The cities and ports of Liverpool and Manchester have always been in many ways interdependent. They shared the prosperity of the boom years. They shared in the post war slump in cotton, a slump which like that in coal was not due entirely to bad international trade conditions, but of the rivalry of an alternative textile material—synthetic silk. Lancashire, however, instead of stolidly standing by, and waiting for cotton to boom again quickly established its own synthetic silk factories and mills, and the textile trade was getting well on to its feet again at the outbreak of the present war.

Liverpool has grown since the days of my ecstatic truant holiday, but not unrecognisably so. The transference of the big Atlantic passenger service was a blow to her pride as well as to her pocket, but she is still Great Britain's second seaport with a huge passenger and merchandise, Atlantic and world-wide trade. And her importance in this respect has not diminished with the war, nor is it likely to do when peace comes, for the ties that have always united her with the Americas and the Empire will be stronger than ever.

Preston and Fleetwood are the only other seaports of Lancashire. Preston actually closer to coal " cotton " than Liverpool, might have been a serious rival ; might even have been Lancashire's premier seaport, had not Liverpool as it were, got in first. The estuary of the River Ribble if enclosed and dredged might have made a very fine harbour. As

41

it is her docks are used chiefly for coastal and canal traffic, handling coal and her own extensive manufactures. Fleetwood is a fishing port with a large fleet of steam trawlers and drifters. She has fish docks of modern design, comparable with those at Hull and Grimsby, with which ports she has been in ever-growing competition since the end of the last war.

We are leaving coal as we go north towards the mountainous regions of Westmorland. But just inside the borders of North Lancashire on the north extremity of Morecambe Bay, there are extremely rich deposits of haematite, a high-grade type of iron ore superior to that of the north-east of England. With coal available by a short sea-passage from north Lancashire and also from Cumberland, this gave rise to a great iron and steel smelting industry concentrated at Barrow-in-Furness which in 1840 was a small fishing village, and is now one of Great Britain's foremost shipyards. It has commercial docks too, with an export trade similar to that of Middlesbrough and an import trade in Irish cattle, coal, of course, and timber. Haematite is found, too, higher up the Westmorland and Cumberland coast, and also coal which in places is actually mined under the sea. But although there are furnaces at Worthington, the two other ports of Cumberland, Whitehaven and Maryport export most of their coal and iron ore to Barrow. As with Liverpool and Preston, Barrow got ahead in the race for industrial development, and the better "natural" harbour was more easily adapted for dock-building than those on the exposed coast.

We come to Scotland again. There are many small seaports and potential commercial harbours along the coasts of Dumfries, Kirkcudbright, Wigtown and southern Ayr, but all these counties again are agricultural in their main activities. There is no coal or concentrations of population until we reach the north part of Ayrshire and the mouth of the Clyde, the western boundary of the industrial belt of lowland Scotland which, as we have seen, extends from the Firth of Forth and owes its prosperity primarily to coal. Greenock, Dumbarton, Port Glasgow are the ports of the Clyde, with Glasgow herself holding undisputed place as the first port of Scotland.

In many ways the commercial history of Glasgow is like that of Liverpool. Little more than a hundred years ago the Clyde was practically unnavigable, and its potentialities were not realised until the growth of its inland coal-fed industries demanded an ocean outlet to the west, and an inlet for the commodites of the New World, raw materials, tobacco and sugar. Glasgow's first ships were sail. But she was as quick as the Tyne to realise the advantages of steam, and as she had the coal and iron she built steamships herself. Indeed, the first real steamship, the *Charlotte Dundas*, was built at Glasgow, and so was the first ocean-going steamship, the *Comet*; here, too, the first steamship dock was built by Napier and thus were laid the foundations of an industry which at Clydebank had

H.M.S. *ILLUSTRIOUS* ENTERING THE BASIN AT JOHN BROWN'S, CLYDEBANK
Drawing by Sir Muirhead Bone

its culmination in the building of the world's two largest passenger ships, *Queen Mary* and *Queen Elizabeth*, and the successful launching of them into a waterway which originally had been little more than a shallow muddy creek. I think that one of the most dramatic and inspiring events in the history of British shipping was that of the launching of the *Queen Elizabeth* by the Queen herself, at a time when the whole world was tense with anxiety as to the outcome of the Munich Conference. I was not an eyewitness of that launch, but I was one of the millions who by radio in this country and overseas heard the Queen in a clear, unfaltering voice make a speech as noble as anything in our language, in which she described the building and the launching of this fine vessel as " an act of faith " ; we heard the smashing of the bottle of wine, the creak and groan, the splintering of wood, the rattling of great chains, and then a dull roar like that of an avalanche as the hull moved down the slip to the water, a roar that was drowned by that of the tumultuous cheers of the men who had built her. . . .

But if shipbuilding was (and is) the chief industry of Glasgow, she is a great manufacturing town, her industries ranging from cotton, jute and linen goods, to paper, glass, light and heavy machinery, and, of course, brewing and the distilling of whisky. In peace time the value of her exports exceeds that of her imports : her imports being raw cotton, jute, grain, timber, tobacco, edible and combustible oils and fats, leather and food stuffs. Her trade is preponderantly with the United States and Canada, but ranges over the entire world. Glasgow, too, has an important ocean passenger trade, but principally in ships that carry cargo too. Greenock, closer to the sea than Glasgow, also has shipyards, but its principal home trade is sugar-refining with the import of which in the raw state most of its shipping is concerned, although it has also a fairly big fishing industry.

The interior of Scotland becomes mountainous north-west of the valley of the Clyde. There is no more coal, and even agriculture can be carried on only in the narrow valleys. Communication by road or rail is difficult. The population is sparse, and becomes sparser as we go north to Ross, Cromarty, Sutherland and Caithness the starting point of our survey. There are in the north-west and extreme north coasts of Scotland scores of sheltered, deep-water lochs for whose natural facilities the builders, say, of London's port, would have paid millions. Yet apart from Fort William, at the west end of the Caledonian Canal, the coast is barren save for small fishing villages and ports, and even these are few and far between, although Stornoway is an important West Highland port and Kirkwall and Lerwick are fishing ports for the Orkneys and Shetlands. Coal in the history of Great Britain's seaports has indeed been king.

VI

SEAPORTS and harbours cannot be mass-produced. Each one we have mentioned is individual and unlike any other. Yet all, of necessity have something in common, and as the activities of London's port embrace practically every form of shipping activity, she may be taken as typical. Her importance is not directly due to coal. Indirectly it is, for coal is the basic source of our national wealth, and London is the commercial as well as the political capital of England. Here at the very hub of the trade routes of the world are concentrated the great banks and financial and insurance houses without which international trade with all its complexities could not be carried on. Here are the ambassadors, the chief consuls, the commercial agents of foreign countries : here are the head executive offices of the great British shipping and railway companies, and the agents of almost every important trading concern in the world. London herself is a great manufacturing town, but above all she is a *market* in which every conceivable grown or manufactured commodity eaten or used by mankind is bought or sold, from

BLACK LION WHARF, CHELSEA
Etching by J. W. M. Whistler, 1834-1903

wheat and wool and elephant tusks and coconuts, to rare drugs, bananas, diamonds, margarine, carpets, wine, platinum, books and locomotives. Most of these are imported, and are unloaded in London's Docks. Most of them are for home consumption, by the twenty million people who live and work within the economic distributive area of the port. But a big proportion of the goods that flow from all parts of the world to London's market are re-shipped to other countries, and by virtue of her own manufactures and by the fact that she is the focusing point of every rail and road transport system of England, the balance of export with import is maintained.

The Port of London includes the whole of the tidal portion of the Thames from Teddington Lock in Middlesex to an imaginary line drawn from Havengore Creek in Essex to Warden Point in Kent, a distance of nearly seventy miles. But the river is not navigable for ocean-going ships higher than London Bridge, and apart from Tilbury, the docks are concentrated on both banks of the Thames between Tower Bridge and Woolwich. That part of the river between London Bridge and Tower Bridge, known as the Upper Pool of London is tidal and is used principally by coastal and small continental steamers loading or discharging direct on to river wharves or overside into river barges. On the north side

45

proceeding down river from Tower Bridge are first of all St. Katherine Docks and London Docks, which include the famous Execution Dock, where pirates, including Captain Kidd, were hanged in chains at low water for three tides. These docks are small and are used by moderate-sized vessels engaged in the coast and continental import trades : marble, olive oil and silk from Italy ; fruit, wines and fresh vegetables and sardines from France, Spain and Portugal ; and manufactured articles and provisions from Belgium. But goods discharged from large vessels lower down the river are brought here by lighters and by road for storage in the immense warehouses that surround the docks. Nowhere else in the world will you see such a variety of goods : wool, hides and rare furs, wines, spirits, spices, sugar, rubber, Rattan canes, tallow, cutch, gums, drugs, essences, coffee, cocoa, tea, iodine, mercury, canned fruit and fish, hemp and coconuts and elephant tusks. The warehouses used for wool alone cover forty acres !

Next on the north bank between the loop in the river called The Isle of Dogs are the West India and Millwall Docks. The West India Docks were the first cargo docks to be built on the banks of the Thames and they were designed for the West Indian sugar trade originally borne in large sailing vessels. To-day sugar is still the principal import, along with molasses and rum, and fruit and other products of the West Indies. But the West Indies Dock system is also the chief centre of the London hardwood trade which includes mahogany, teak, ebony, jarrah, walnut, rosewood, cedar and boxwood. The Millwall Docks have a more general trade with the raw and semi-raw and manufactured goods of North and South America, the Baltic, North and West Africa and Russia. The East India Docks lie between the West India and the Royal Victoria and Albert and King George, and they are equipped for dealing with general import and export cargoes ; the Royal Albert and King George form the biggest and most modern dock system on the north bank of the Thames and it is here that the chief trade in Australian and New Zealand wool and frozen meat and dairy products is centred. But the activities of these docks cover practically every type of cargo and ship. In normal times as many as fifty large vessels may be berthed in them simultaneously ; huge cargo ships, tankers, and passenger liners from America, South Africa, India, China and Japan. Here on the dock side are the three largest flour mills in London handling grain direct from ships' holds and discharging it as bags of flour into trains and fleets of lorries, or barges or small coastal ships for re-export. Here comes a large proportion of the tobacco that is consumed, not only by Great Britain, but by the smokers of many European countries. Here are cold storage warehouses one of which can hold as many as 250,000 carcases of New Zealand mutton. And from these docks, too, sail fast passenger liners to nearly every maritime country of the world.

THE FIRST SATURDAY OF THE BLITZ : THE PORT OF LONDON, 1940
Oil painting by E. Boye Uden

On the south bank of the Thames between Rotherhithe and the Isle of Dogs, is another vast system of Docks known collectively as the Surrey Commercial, and as its name implies it has a general trade, but it specialises in soft-wood timber, and actually handles thirty per cent. of the whole of Great Britain's annual imports (nearly 2,500,000 tons). Most of this is fir, pine and spruce from North America, Scandinavia and Russia, and importers store it at the Docks until required by the market. For this purpose there are special sheds covering 77 acres, and open storage grounds sufficient to store half-a-million tons of timber.

Each of these dock systems would alone serve for a port of considerable size, but farther down the river are the Tilbury Docks, still under the authority of the P.L.A., and an integral and indispensable part of the port itself. They were opened in the year 1886, but since then have been greatly extended and improved until, with the building of a floating landing stage (similar to that of Liverpool) and a large graving dock, Tilbury is the finest dock system in the world, capable of handling all but the largest of the Atlantic super-liners. Tilbury, indeed, because of its nearness to the sea, has captured much of the West India Dock passenger trade. From here, liners sail to the Far East, South Africa, North and South America as regularly as the Atlantic mails from Southampton, but, of course, it can never compete seriously either with Southampton or Liverpool in the direct express New York service. Its commercial docks have a general business comparable with that of the West India, but Tilbury is also a port of call with vessels discharging or taking only a part cargo.

While London (with her average pre-war arrivals and departures of ships more than 62,000) is undoubtedly Great Britain's greatest seaport, and probably the greatest seaport in the world, it would be unfair to say that she is more modern and go-ahead than the other big ports we have mentioned in this survey. Her docks are triumphs of engineering as is the deepening and widening of her waterways and their seaward approaches. But the same applies to Southampton, Liverpool, Glasgow, Hull and Newcastle. Her docks are equipped with marvellous machinery for the handling of ships, for the expeditious loading and discharging and storage of cargoes. There are cranes—electric and hydraulic ; there are suction plants for discharging grain ; conveyors and lifts for bananas and frozen meat ; bunkering apparatus both for coal and oil. There are special warehouses for grain, meat, fruit, wines and tobacco. But most of these exist, too, at the other ports. The truth is that all these ports are cogs in the huge machine by which our island nation exists. Small wonder then that an enemy bent on our national destruction has done his utmost to smash the cogs and bring the machine to a standstill. But those cogs are forged of something stronger than British steel : of British character. The harm done to our great and little seaports by ruthless air-bombing has been immense in lives and material. But the cogs have never ceased to turn ; and the machine, instead of slowing down, has moved at a greater pace. Bombs on their own homes as well as on the harbours have not deterred our dockers from carrying on the vital work of loading and off-loading the ships by which we eat and fight, any more than mines and U-boats and air attacks have deterred the sailors themselves in their hazardous voyages. Dock railwaymen, motor transport drivers, dock police (ashore and afloat), the fire-fighting services, the demolition and salvage squads, the civilian and naval port executive staffs have combined in a cool defiance of the enemy's frightfulness designed as much as anything to destroy morale. The Battle of Britain has been and will be, until Nazism is destroyed utterly, the Battle of our Seaports. And so far the seaports have won.